Regrets Only

Regrets Only:
Contemporary Poets on the Theme of Regret

edited by
Martha Manno

Little Pear Press
Seekonk, MA

Little Pear Press
Seekonk, MA 02771
www.littlepearpress.com
© 2006 by Martha Manno
All rights reserved
Book design by Christina Gruppuso
Printed in the USA
ISBN: 0-9746-9111-9
ISBN 13: 978-0-9746-9111-4

Acknowledgements:
Prairie Schooner for "Ripe" and *Beloit Poetry* for "What It Was," by Roy Jacobstein
Fireweed for "Pol Pot's Wife Talks To Whoever Will Listen" by Willa Schneberg
Light Year and *The Bedford Introduction to Literature* for "The Lover Not Taken" by Blanche Farley
New Zoo Poetry Review for "Twenty-five Years Of Rejection Slips" and *One Trick Pony* for "Saying Good-Bye" by Barbara Crooker
Bend Bulletin for "At Last Safe Arbor" by Kake Huck
Lichen for "The Shiverin' Bits" by Rhoda Janzen
Riverside Quarterly and *Three Genres* for "Regret" by Judy Kronenfeld
Roanoke Review for "Service" by Judith H. Montgomery
Bay Windows for "Fairy Tales for Writers: Sleeping Beauty" and *STAR*LINE* for "Free Books" by Lawrence Schimel

For P, C & N with no regrets

Poetry is the clear expression of mixed feelings.
—W. H. Auden

There is no one, no matter how wise he is, who has not in his youth said things or done things that are so unpleasant to recall in later life that he would expunge them entirely from his memory if that were possible.
—Marcel Proust

Table of Contents

Yellow	*Elizabeth Stabler*	13
Once Upon a Time	*Ruth Mark*	14
Ripe	*Roy Jacobstein*	16
At the Edge of the Empty Nest	*Jessica G. de Koninck*	17
Before the Astronauts Came	*Lee Glantz*	18
What Is True in This Story	*Margo Solod*	19
Rendezvous	*Meg Petersen*	20
Pol Pot's Wife Talks to Whoever Will Listen	*Willa Schneberg*	21
Regret, Like Thursday After Lunch	*Kake Huck*	23
She Sees	*Amanda Surkont*	24
Twenty-five Years of Rejection Slips	*Barbara Crooker*	25
The Deer	*Deborah Narin-Wells*	26
Whale Watching	*Julie R. Enszer*	28
Free Books	*Lawrence Schimel*	30
Robert Frost's Backyard, Derry	*Helen Marie Casey*	31
The Fittest	*Gary J. Whitehead*	32
What It Was	*Roy Jacobstein*	35
Winter in Juniper Hill Cemetery	*Elizabeth Stabler*	36
The Lover Not Taken	*Blanche Farley*	37
Buddha, the Father	*Carly Sachs*	38
When She Leaves	*Dianne Stepp*	39
To All a Good Night	*James Cihlar*	41
A Puny Rescuer	*Cecelia Hagen*	42
Happy Birthday, Baby	*Helen Ruggieri*	43
Working Wonders	*Davi Walders*	45
Message for Augustine	*Jane D'Arista*	46
The Hunger Artist	*Barbara Schweitzer*	47
Saying Good-bye	*Barbara Crooker*	48
Regret	*Judy Kronenfeld*	49
A Thought Late In Summer (Paris, France)	*Louis Bourgeois*	50

Lost and Found	Elizabeth Stabler	51
I Want to Be a Man	Cecelia Hagen	54
Service	Judith H. Montgomery	56
Kent, Ohio	Carly Sachs	57
Diet Man	Angela D'Arista Solli	58
Feedback as Requested	Elizabeth Whyman	59
The Great Blue Heron Is a...	V. T. Abercrombie	60
What The Dead Do	Cher Holt-Fortin	61
My Debt to the Moon	Meg Petersen	62
Empty Nest	Chris Waters	63
Holidays	Nancy Collins Boardman	64
Blue	Chella Courington	65
On the Anniversary of Your Death	Helen Marie Casey	66
I Am Reminded When Thinking	Andrena Zawinski	67
The Shiverin' Bits	Rhoda Janzen	69
Requiem for a Close Friend	Kamilah Aisha Moon	71
Dead Branches	Lisa McMann	72
The Poem I Did Not Write	Jessica G. de Koninck	73
Woman with Fevers	Christopher Woods	75
Mourner's Kaddish, a Variation	Carly Sachs	77
Doorway	Jeremy Farrington	78
The Spendthrift Heart	Barbara Schweitzer	79
On Algebra Test Mornings	Audrey Friedman	80
The Shell Game	V.T. Abercrombie	81
Father's Mission	Laurence J. Sasso Jr.	82
Seventeen	Elizabeth Thomas	83
Churn	Lisa McMann	85
Delia D., 1970	Suzanne Sigafoos	86
Bed Cats	Kathryn Kulpa	87
Anna Claire	Chella Courington	88
Birthday Party	Jeremy Farrington	90
Last Words	Pat Hegnauer	91
Ocean Isle Beach, 1964	Elizabeth Scism	92
I Still Have Everything You Gave Me	Margo Solod	93
Fairy Tales for Writers: Sleeping Beauty	Lawrence Schimel	94

Despite Cancer and the Ohio Winter Mother Insists I Drive Her to Visit Lila's New Baby	Suzanne Sigafoos	95
Note from a Motel	Andrena Zawinski	96
Jeans	Elizabeth Whyman	97
Mission	Michele F. Cooper	98
List	Joyce Sakala	100
Of the Liquid Trees	Louis E. Bourgeois	101
Raccoon	Cecelia Hagen	102
Broker	N.M. Brewka	103
Letter from the Shore	Lin Nulman	105
Absent	Helen Marie Casey	107
Thinsulated	Barbara Schweitzer	108
Invitation #2	Alice Friman	110
Regret	Shulla Sannella	111
Deus ex Machina	Pat Hegnauer	112
Cherubs	Teresa Joy Kramer	113
2 A.M.	Suzy Lamson	114
A Journey from Rhode Island to Florida	Catherine McCrane Keating	115
Requiem for Judith Resnick	Davi Walders	116
Looking Backward	Ada Jill Schneider	118
Ali, Short for Alexandra	Ruth Bailey	119
Expedition	James Cihlar	120
Can Anyone Spell "Indecision"?	Shelley Ann Wake	122
The End of the Daughters of Minyas	Susan Firghil Park	124
The Drawer	Kathleen Kirk	125
This Time Will Not Come Again	Ruth Mark	126
The Rich Historian	Valerie Russo	127
Saying Goodbye	Barbara Crooker	129
At Last Safe Harbor	Kake Huck	130
Contributors		131
About the Editor		141

Elizabeth Stabler

Yellow

Cold yellow rain streams through the lindens
blurs a notice of sudden death—
At once you are here, othertime friend
and as soon, taken away
leaving beaten branches hung in yellow
and the salt of stalled love, fresh sorrow.

A sodden pile forms a book of hours—
this leaf tagged happy green rush,
these many, yellow slow down.
Noncommitment was bond and boundary:
the hard words sting and pool at my feet,
wash over stale glancings, faint good-byes.

I met your damn drummer, saw you march off
to other loves, distant stations.
But why that far treeless place? And to die there?
Yellow falls soft over yellow
blankets the soaked earth, prepares the bed.
Come home, lie where the yellow tulips wait.

Ruth Mark

Once Upon a Time

Once it was nothing to spend all
day at play by the stream,
or making mud pies 'til the
sun baked them dry. Normal to splash in
the surf at Waterfoot, the taste
of the briny water
the salt of dulse in concentration.

Once it seemed to stay sunny
all summer long, only smell of
autumn, leaves, mulch and
coal-smoke fumes when it turned
September and was time to return
once more to school, with books like
bricks and coats too long for us.

Then it was the norm to hit a tennis
ball against the side of the
house, practicing for Wimbledon
in my head, until Dad went
up for his afternoon kip and the
thumping would have to stop for
an hour or two only to resume
until tea-time or night fall.

Now I measure the days in
lists of *things to do*, accomplishments,
the next job, the next stack
of laundry, the next paper
to mark. I long to lay down
the guilt I've acquired in adulthood—
the guilt bought from doing nothing, just *being*
gazing at beauty, sea, mountains, grass,
endless sky for as long as it takes to
achieve nothing but peace,
which I could then use to
bury the guilt, embrace
the child in me once more.

Roy Jacobstein

Ripe

Somewhere my father must be
eating the *mooshy* parts of a peach
as a favor for a child,
the way he once did for me.
May it be sunny there, and a lei
of light illumine his brow.
The years it's taken to learn sweetness
resides in the bruises.

Jessica G. de Koninck

At the Edge of the Empty Nest

Forty-five
My teenaged daughter
Runs breathless
Into our house.
Refrigerator open,
She stops.
Turns to me
Eyes wide,
It's true, she says
My friends joke
I look just like you.
Could you get a different haircut?

Twenty-nine
I am ironing
Tiny white undershirts
In the second floor walkup
We rent in Belleville.
I am ironing
Tiny yellow booties
So everything will be ready
For this baby
For whom I will never
Be ready.
If time permits
I will go get my hair cut.

Lee Glantz

Before the Astronauts Came

I want you, Moon, to assume
the position you held yesterday.

I want you, Moon,
to remain the same.

Before the astronauts came
you were not composed

of the stuff our dustpans eat
on planet Earth.

Since those brave men proved
your magic promise bare,

musicians and poets
find only indifference in your face.

The dog, the wolf, and I
have no reason to ululate.

I want you, Moon, to assume the position
you held before you were besmirched,

stripped of speculation,
and true lunacy.

Margo Solod

What Is True in This Story

The gold plastic loving cup filled with new pennies,
broken, the treasure scattered before it
could be awarded. The way a print of Van Gogh's
Sunflowers brings the taste of a blue gumball to my tongue,
another prize, this one for brain and not for body. How
the scent of lavender still makes me wince, remembering
a long dead teacher who expected more from me than I
could bother with. I made her cry. She might have been
in love with me though she would never call it that. What
is true is some nights I can't sleep:

I broke it, stole it, borrowed it,
ruined it. I didn't care,
never got there, just forgot. I never
talked about it, never said it,
meant it, lied about it.
I wasn't there.

Rendezvous

Outside Filene's, Mall of New Hampshire,
late November, you pull up to the curb
in a maroon Mercury with New York plates.
You are dressed entirely in black.
As we embrace, I feel you gather substance
as if coming back to yourself,
until being in my own bones and blood
become real to me.

Our words rush over each other greedily,
and yet we are loathe to spend them.
We select from the richness
of all we didn't know we had to say
until the other came to hear it.

I know what it is to live
in a place that starves you slowly
until you wonder if you still exist behind
the life you carry on.
We both know how the weight
of your art can be the anchor,
that holds you to this world.

Our 90 minutes evaporate like the vapor in our breath,
and you return me to Filenes's curb,
and while the motor on your rental car still runs, and
under a full moon, of course, with my hand on the door latch,
you tell me you have loved me from the first instant
and through 25 years of moments since.

Some truth is invaluable, some just painful—
I'm not sure about this one.
I watch you pull away;
your taillights bleed
into the enveloping darkness.

Willa Schneberg

Pol Pot's Wife Talks to Whoever Will Listen

Khieu Ponnary is going mad in the service of her husband's revolution.—Elizabeth Becker

I
Before the corpses,
Sar kissed my fingertips
and clung to my every word
as if they had wings
and could fly him to a black pajama Utopia.

In Keng Vannsak's apartment
on St. Andres des Arts
I flirted with Sar in French.
I knew everything:
Stalin's tract "On The National Question,"
Lenin's "On Imperialism."
Talking revolution was sexy.
I would brush against Sar's shoulder
and whisper "Destroy the bourgeoisie,
re-educate the masses."

II
Before I pretended words were white
lotus flowers in cloisonné vases,
declawed cats or impotent men,
but they have always been murderous,

Pol Pot locked me in this house.
Sar would never allow this.
He will come and stroke my hair and
tell me no one is dying,

but the corpses won't let me sleep.
They curse me, press into me—
inseminate me with their agony.

My words want to wear gray pinafores
as I did in the French Lycée,
but can only don black—
the color of the world.

Kake Huck

Regret, Like Thursday After Lunch

broke open my bowl of sky.
I held your gaze two beats
too long, seeking what ease

desires of energy. That look
told everything. And nothing.
Unuttered questions glazed

my tongue. Heat and light
restrained. Cloud fingers
pressed toward evening—

my hands
could not span the table.

Nothing fell into Thursday
like the squall that soaked
our desert, dying into sun
by dusk.

Amanda Surkont

She Sees

An old man with nothing.
He tends to things
in the garden things
nobody wants to eat.
She thinks his pants
too old and too soft.
As soft as his mind
these days. She recalls
she loved him once
when she was ten
and the other girls
in the building were
without fathers.

Barbara Crooker

Twenty-five Years of Rejection Slips,

and what does it matter? How many trees have been pulped
for this constant susurrus: sending, resending,
  shuffling, sorting?
Even the name *submission* suggests a certain deference,
servility, prostration: lying down in front of the mailbox,
and letting the great steamroller of indifference flatten
me into the ground. You could read the morning newspaper
through my bones. Maybe here is the lesson: Look
at the wind, how it turns the pages of the leaves, riffles
through chapter after chapter, whispers countless stories
that no one bothers to write down. Look at the stanzas
of light in the locust leaves as they bob and weave
in the hot July wind, their effortless green repetition
and refrain. Why not give it up now? The phone isn't going
to ring; the mailbox is full of circulars and bills. So maybe
I'll read to the cardinals and wrens, sink back in the hammock,
listen to the hot buzz of the cicadas' applause.
Look, clouds are writing their manuscripts on the big blue book
of the sky. They don't fear the wind's erasure, or night's
emphatic black rejection. Tomorrow, a clean sheet comes up
in the roller, and we'll start all over again.

Deborah Narin-Wells

The Deer

I feel him watch me
at the sink scrubbing dishes
as if, my hands shiny with soap,
I've summoned him here,
his kneeling body half hidden
in the winter-white heather,
the breath blowing from his mouth
like puffs of smoke
from the woodstove.
He isn't afraid
when I move room to room;
to him I'm only a shadow
appearing, disappearing.

I wonder at his vastness,
the antlers climbing
like a ladder to the sky.

Sometimes his whole body trembles
the way light trembles on the rhododendron
and I worry he's come here to die.
I imagine the dark wet leaves
beneath his belly
as he tries to raise himself up,
legs collapsing like a broken chair,
and the terrible sound
like that of birds who,
mistaking our living room for home,
slam into the sliding glass door.

I speak to him then. I tell him
ever since I was a child
I've loved him. I want to reach out
my hand, touch the space
between his antlers
like touching the stars.
He doesn't answer.
He has no use for my compassion.
Or is it fear?

He knows the soul leaves the body
as easily as this rain
running down the trees.

Julie R. Enszer

Whale Watching

There was a time when I could recite complete passages from
Mary Oliver:
"There is all around us this country of original fire. You know
what I mean."
We traveled to Provincetown, a party of ten—
you and I with the second most longevity.

"There is all around us this country of original fire. You know
what I mean,"
together two and a half years,
you and I with the second most longevity.
We went whale watching.

Together two and a half years,
into Stellwagen Bay, "off the cape,"
we went whale watching
with seventy-odd tourists all peering off the side of the boat.

In Stellwagen Bay, "off the cape,"
wind ripped through our hair; I was sick from the sun.
With seventy-odd tourists all peering off the side of the boat,
we saw them: a gaggle of whales.

Wind ripped through our hair; I was sick from the sun.
We watched, captivated.
We saw them. A gaggle of whales.
Each breeched and logged and pec slapped.

I watched captivated;
you took pictures throughout
each breeching and logging and pec slapping;
I hope your Kodak caught the whole show.

You took pictures throughout the
afternoon. Clicked through the trip.
I hope your Kodak caught the whole show.
I would never know. We broke up two days

after. At noon. It clicked. Through the trip.
I hope your pictures are as vivid as my memories.
I would never know. We broke up. Two days
later. I still remember the whales.

I hope your pictures are as vivid as my memories—
we traveled to Provincetown, a party of ten.
Later still I remember the whales.
There was a time when I could recite complete passages from
Mary Oliver.

Lawrence Schimel

Free Books

I had not thought my sign was open to interpretation.
My neighbors, walking down our street, stopped
before the box I'd left and browsed among
my duplicates, the gifts of friends, the books
I'd bought but did not read, the ones I'd never read again.
Even if they did not select a volume, they all agreed
it was a great idea. But then, Cambridge is a bookish
town; we all had too many books in too little space.
They quickly emerged from their homes again
with armloads of their own no-longer-wanteds,
tomes they'd been assigned in school or books their children
had outgrown, inscribed chapbooks from readings
they'd attended only as a favor to a friend—
whatever their reasons for getting rid of them,
they brought them down the street to my box
of free books, as if I'd been asking for them
instead of giving away. I began to know
the frustration Hercules felt each time he chopped off
one of the Hydra's heads, and two more grew
to take its place. Stormclouds rumbled overhead,
and I, no child of the gods, admitted my mortal defeat
and carried the box, now filled with even more books
than when I'd started, inside before the rains fell.

Helen Marie Casey

Robert Frost's Backyard, Derry

He is not home today. I walk out
where the stillness is. Dried leaves
are voices underfoot, trees coming
undone, the world changing clothes.
His shade may be about, eyeing the apples.
He cannot like it now, the noise that rumbles
down the highway, intruders in his backyard,
admirers nosing at his windows, strangers,
a dad and a boy, pitching baseball-sized apples,
lopsided and pocked, toward a fading sky.

Gary J. Whitehead

The Fittest

—for Sam, in the hope that you'll be fitter

And so he comes with his thumbs
and dumb luck, his hunger hoisted
by the first rope of smoke off
a four-legged thing charred
by heat lightning's quick, thin hand.

Crossing glades and continents,
fucking and chucking spears at
anything that moves, he uses
and consumes and hoofs it across
the ice in search of bigger things.

Footsteps like a language spelled
out across an epoch. His back sore
from so much bending over, he stands
up straight, parks himself for a time
on a continent despite the ice.

He tethers a toothy, wire-haired
smiler and utters, "dog." Okay,
maybe it isn't just him hooked
on the broth of sloth, blasted on
chops of mastodon, penetrating pell—

mell the armor of the armadillo's cousin
(the glyptodont). But glyphs don't lie.
They're ancient artsy-fartsy smoking
guns. It was cold for a while, sure,
but when has a little frost ever wiped

out an elephant in a wool sweater,
or a cat for that matter, one with big
teeth? So he likes his meat and women—
and so much so that after forty billion
more steps—through the Pleistocene

and into the Holocene—he wakes
one morning, farts, lights a Marlboro,
dumps Fruit Loops in a bowl,
and reads The New York Times
in his giant parquet wood-floored cave,

annoyed to hear the lawn mower
of another biped pacing across
a thirty-yard tract of grass.
Pan out, camera. Check out
the morning meal of North America,

the clear-cut flora eaten down
to the bowl, nothing but roads
and industry and homes and malls
swirled in the toxic milk
of fumes and solid waste;

where sandwiches are served in neat,
roomy red and yellow bags;
where whatever fresh kills aren't shat
down pipes get dumped in huge piles
in the freshwater wetlands;

where somewhere the ivory-billed
woodpecker may or may not haunt
the swamps of Louisiana; place
where the passenger pigeon, once
numbering three to five billion,

the most abundant bird on the planet,
no longer coos in the branches.
Have you heard of the last wild one?
On March 4th, 1900, it was shot dead
by a boy, 14, in Pike County, Ohio.

But it wasn't the last passenger.
The last, Martha, named for Washington's
wife, curled her claws once and for all
in the Cincinnati Zoo at 12:30 p.m.
on September 1st, 1914, at the very

moment that Darwin's dust twitched
beneath the cold stones of Westminster.
But who cares? There's school today.
And hunger and love and rage.
There's a heavy, heavy pair of boots

plodding on into the age. And now
the Fruit Loops have turned to mush,
and I'm reading all this through a ring
of spilled milk spreading on the page.

Roy Jacobstein

What It Was

Often, at Strong Memorial Hospital,
I'd guide a 15-gauge needle into the center
of a child's lower back. It was so easy,
any time I wanted I could slip it in,
between the vertebral ridges of L2 and L3,
blindfolded even, feel the pop, and presto—
cerebrospinal fluid dripping out. I never could
get the nurses to believe the kid
did not have acute leukemia. They knew
the drill: slap on the purple label,
call the stat messenger, console the parents
waiting for the test results, a flotilla
of 100,000 deranged cells per cubic centimeter
pouring from Mona's marrow or Phil's spleen
into the bloodstream. After my latest 36-hour day,
sun risen, set, risen, set, I'd arrive home,
smelling of night rattles and slow clocks
and sodden scrambled eggs, and slip
into my then-wife's arms, wanting only
to be told what it wasn't. But all she said
before I went under, swimming her reefs
without aqualung or mask, was what it was.

Elizabeth Stabler

Winter in Juniper Hill Cemetery

Four puffs of down blaze
high in the bare azalea
come there from a mat of moss and leaves
fresh-pawed for a winter meal

where they lay soft by a broken fan
of gray/white feathers
and lone blood-tipped quill
torn from the syrinx of last summer's clown

who rehearsed his concert of borrowed tunes
all morning on the high antenna
bouncing up up with glee after each number
making antic bows to quiet sparrows.

On the swaying branch where buds show pink
four shreds still bloom, silence around.

Blanche Farley

The Lover Not Taken

Committed to one, she wanted both
And, mulling it over, long she stood,
Alone on the road, loath
To leave, wanting to hide in the undergrowth.
This new guy, smooth as a yellow wood

Really turned her on. She liked his hair,
His smile. But the other, Jack, had a claim
On her already and she had to admit, he did wear
Well. In fact, to be perfectly fair,
He understood her. His long, lithe frame

Beside hers in the evening tenderly lay.
Still, if this blond guy dropped by someday,
Couldn't way just lead on to way?
No. For if way led on and Jack
Found out, she doubted if he would ever come back.

Oh, she turned with a sigh.
Somewhere ages and ages hence,
She might be telling this. "And I— "
She would say, "stood faithfully by."
But by then who would know the difference?

With that in mind, she took the fast way home,
The road by the pond, and phoned the blond.

Buddha, the Father

One day I will wake up
& you will have left your shoes by the door.
I will know you have gone, but not left.
I will have to tell the children
that their father lives in the wind & in the river,
but he has left his shoes.
We will all take turns walking in them.
We will find you in the living room,
at McDonald's, in Nepal.
You will send us necklaces of glass
& maps drawn on dollar bills.
We will answer you by blowing poems out the window.
We will throw salt from the roof
& climb the trees in the front yard.
When we feel like just sitting,
I will read them the poems I have written about you.
I want them to know
that their father saves ducks,
waters the plants
& sings when he pisses.

Dianne Stepp

When She Leaves

she carries off five books and the clothes
on her back, or is it six?
It doesn't matter. She cradles them
like an infant in her arms, cheered
by the flush of their muted spines.

In the photograph she leaves behind
her husband looks like a nestling, a baby owl,
bewildered, his moustaches,
his feathery wisps of hair, and she, pressing
her cheek against his, she is the warmth
he leans his heart against.

There's no point speaking of plans,
as she steps across the curb, or of the dozer
lurching up the street. No point
saying that the color of the cottage
on the corner changes from red to gray,
or that the Doberman charges the gabled gate
snarling horribly.

The point is the morning glory
comes 'round the picket to offer its blueness,
the creamy trumpet of its throat,
and Queen Anne's Lace grows rampant
in the ditch beside the broken bricks.

One way or another a window
will open, a curtain
graze her arm.
There will be bookends
fashioned from yellow pine or cedar,
myrtlewood, or even granite
for that matter cold as it may be.
And O roses of course in a blue

vase, and in the garden,
pushing through spring soil,
sweet mallow and cornlilies.

James Cihlar

To All a Good Night

Our father, who is not dying,
my language is smaller than you.

In fields below the mountains,
low blocks of light search for fruit.

Eliot—is this dull?
A yellow flower on the wall,

it screams "James."
I don't dare. I don't care.

Heaven must be another place
with long waiting lines,

shucked clamshells, robins,
Christmas by the shore.

Fresh peach makes the devil his own.
How am I going to get there?

Once you've gone textbook,
there's no turning back.

Let the meadow follow
the horses galloping loose.

It has a lengthy decision to make.
Bring us back to our daily bed,

tuck us in there, tight,
sprout whiskers on our heads.

Cecelia Hagen

A Puny Rescuer

I thought you the great in all things, in guilt
and in glory. You're but a puny.—James Joyce

Smoke chokes the staircase.
I dash back in
to save the children,
their soft feet dangling
over my arm, my body

their shield. We huddle
together and watch
as the rafters sag.
I know I caused the fire,
let a small candle

from my youth go on burning
too long until I,
the hero, the puny, got
everyone out and was
praised for the rescue.

They're bringing me coffee
and patting my back
and I don't explain
how I let the fire start,
I can't even remember

the match that was struck
to light the candle
that started this blaze,
a roaring accuser
that points back at me,

careless dissembler,
restless tender of flames.

Helen Ruggieri

Happy Birthday, Baby

We had an agreement about our birthdays.
First me, two days later, you.
Wherever we were—you'd call and rub it in.
We'd exchange outlines of our lives:
your current wife, motorcycle,
my newest baby, my latest plot.

On the 30th, I waited all day.
Only the insurance man remembered.
I slipped over alone, so mature
I reasoned it was foolish to count
on twenty year old promises.

I imagined you driving a car,
of all things, losing your hair,
the swagger gone out of you.
already dull like everyone else.

I don't know why we were friends,
why we loved ideas more, talked
as if what we loved was each other.
Now middle aged we had no clique
to close ourselves off from.

At 40, the dentist sent a card.
I stayed in the same place
so you'd know where to find me.
I remembered you walking down the hall
striking your cleats on the floor,
leaving a trail of sparks.

I wanted to tell you the high school
burned down, all our records gone.
What's your alibi, Baby, I'd say.
At the reunion, I asked about you.
They said you were dead,
a motorcycle accident, years ago,
hadn't I heard?

The speed was too much for me,
two days spread between us
lurched into decades, and you were
a ghost in a black leather jacket.
I was following a trail of sparks,
prisoner of physics, that class we cut
to smoke down by the tracks.

Motorcycles haven't changed that much,
the Harley's turning 100 this year.
I heard your first wife lives in L.A.,
divorced again, had her face done,
looks great they say.

My plots turn into poems,
fewer these days, but longer.
I want them to go further,
now that I know how
it all comes out.

If I'm fast enough
this poem will be waiting
at the World's Largest Pothole
in Archibald, PA, so when we drive
up in that black '51 Merc
with the chopped top
I'll already know how futile
promises are.

Davi Walders

Working Wonders

So large, so real, so present,
Oseola McCarty might just speak
from the Annie Leibovitz portrait
in the museum gallery. Sweaters
a kilter, hair a crown of uncontrolled
silver, she stares into the camera,
lips set, almost smiling. She stands
in Hattiesburg heat, her yard and
wood-frame house a background blur
behind her large eyes and steady gaze.

So many nevers—never finished
Eureka Elementary, never drove,
never traveled, never explored
or earned more than nine thousand
dollars each of the seventy-five
years she took in laundry before
arthritis crippled her. Washing
each dropped-off bundle, ironing,
folding, tying up her small deposits
week after week, year after year.

And then the decision. Summoning up
from her own deprivation a vision
of determined imagination. Walking
to the bank, making the withdrawal.
The long, slow bus trip across town.
Waiting. Waiting all afternoon
to startle, to hand over one hundred
fifty thousand dollars to Southern Miss.
Waiting to speak, to give, to educate
others. Waiting with that same look
as she stands in her level yard,
her level eyes daring you to cry.

Jane D'Arista

Message for Augustine

I was surprised you were here,
Near the house where I was sent back,
Walking with those who follow you now.
Always before I was told you were coming
And could hide. Now that you are known,
I am known—and know myself—
As Augustine's abandoned concubine,
The fig they say you picked when ripe
And tossed aside to dry.

Believing you would think I sought you out,
I turned away—hiding from what you
Could not help but show. Our life
Is gone from your life—those days
We lived together so easily—
You—kissing my arm, tasting the salt
That excited you. Is that memory gone?
Will I never find my face cradled again
In the softness of your eye?

They say you are changed by love for God,
Drained of self—dead to the life
I have had no wish to survive.
But isn't it selfish to think the past
Is yours alone? To assume that I,
Like our son, have passed from this world?
As you see, I remain—one who wants only
To hear you say the name I sign

_____

Say it.

Barbara Schweitzer

The Hunger Artist

...and they buried the hunger artist, straw and all.—Franz Kafka

I am the hunger artist starving to death,
Kafkaesque and cruel, letting slowly go
of everything that resembles excess
like loving you, my extravagant blow,
but glancing off your cheek, a clucking beam
that might capture a facet of light and change
it to an object with front, back, and seam,
a thread of which might have contained your name
if you had absorbed the ultraviolet.
What happened between us is only grief
and its repository of violence.
Leaving requires no more effort than sleep.
Hay covers the hunger artist in her cage
like disappeared words as you turn the page.

Barbara Crooker

Saying Good-bye

Apparently trivial detail...can show us the world, the beauty to
which we are always, sooner or later, saying good-bye.
—Robert Kelly

October, and the late afternoon sun slants in,
laying down a glaze of gold from the west.
It's time to cut basil, snip and strip
the dark green leaves with their breath
of anise for pesto on a winter night,
when the sky is a lid of polished glass.

It's time to dry oregano, thyme, mint,
to simmer apples and cinnamon, mill them
down to sauce, a rosy reduction.

All summer, I've put up jars of jam:
raspberry, blueberry, blackberry, peach.
They sit smugly in the cellar
like money in the bank, their lids sealed
with such sweet certainty.

One night, a year from now, or twenty, or ten,
one side of this brass bed will be empty, one
pillow undented, one space under the log cabin
quilt smooth as stone. Sooner, or later, one of us
will sleep alone. And all these nights, katydids
arguing their did-nots/did-toos outside the screen,
when sleep takes us before love does, will be long
and black and full of regret.

Judy Kronenfeld

Regret

It's 3:30 on a gray afternoon
late in November.
Winter is homicidal in the air,
a knife-blade at my cheek.
At the apartment door I reach
for the key-string on my neck
and know at once it's gone.
I frisk my school-books, my gym clothes,
my shoes, imagining luck
tricky as an acrobat's timing.
My memory interrogates the day
like a white light in an empty
white room, but won't surprise me
with the key, asleep
in a forgotten pocket.
What I recall, like pictures
of the dead, is the knot,
only double-tied.

There is nothing to do but sit
in the dingy hall, lost in reverie
over the key. It lay like a talisman
on my chest bone, where I am hollow now.
I would give anything for its good weight.
There is nothing to do but think
of past joy. Cannily
it slipped into the lock
and was made for the lock;
beautifully the tumblers turned,
the bolt obeyed.

Louis Bourgeois

A Thought Late In Summer
(Paris, France)

I have grown too old to live among society. I will take my few
meager things and head for the woods. I know of a place not
far from here where there is a pond in the deepest part of the
forest. Hardly anyone knows about it. I will go there and build
a small cabin. There, in total isolation from the brutality of man
and woman, I will exist like a tree, a rock, the stillest pond. I will
think of these forty years of life as a dream lived out to the death by
someone else. The nearness of death is our sweet sonata.

Elizabeth Stabler

Lost and Found

The howl rises   north northeast
great wads of dark   hurtle past—
Body tense, awake to the pull
the thrill the ride face to rain
the need to shed   taste of
your mouth, your hands in
my hair   need to strip
to see over again—
Crouched ashore another self
averse to risk and clutching tight
the cracked vase   pressed rose
afraid to let go
of the be-all and end-all

time before.

Relentless November gale
in hunt of dross and bloat—
Block ears in vain
to stressed groaning limbs
deadwood racket falling—
The fury descends   severs mooring
knot and line   shreds all
that clings and shouts—
Hand torn from hand
the pulse dragooned
dance to the wild banjo
fast faster—

Everything must go—
Take it all!

Jaded ornamental
flaunting late bloom
decapped   in one gust—
Indian summer sap and
dazed insects   flushed
out to the bay—
Autumn slugged in the gut
rotten apple sweetness
fevered flesh   cut by
cold rain—Geese honking
blown out of formation
broken strands of DNA
flying south—

What is left   after?

Bare trunks inked against the
scrubbed sky   and the stripped canopy
its fine-laced fingers reaching up
thick with speech—
The tulip tree lit with ambient light
a candelabra
tall on a table of debris—
Empty nests unveiled   witness
to a once settled place—
The curtain turned back
torn away   to the
bones of things—
To a world beyond ken

power   to unseat the mind.

In the throbbing, brilliant night
the air washed thin
and hard to breathe—
All places of safekeeping
cleansed of burr
and embellishment—
Nerves unsheathed
alert to the faint crackle

and lift
of beaten bracken—
Cold, blue Dog Star rising

The unguarded self.

Cecelia Hagen

I Want to Be a Man

I want to be a man,
to jog along the river at dusk,
to have beefy forearms and fingers
wide as carrots. I want to wear
a baseball hat without the look
of costume, to have it fit
my buzz cut, cover
my secret bald spot.

I want freedom and agony
on a grand scale. When I'm sick,
I want a woman to offer tea and soup.
I want to sink nails in three strokes,
gobble air as I run uphill,
take it into my 18-inch neck,
push it down with my Adam's apple,
feel it spread effectively

throughout my birthright.
I want to have a birthright.
I want to enroll in a women's studies class
to meet a requirement.
I want do some of the reading,
talk in class a lot, voice opinions
with my legs spread wide
on the narrow wooden seat.

Let me steer a wheelbarrow of gravel
evenly down the path, start
the lawnmower with one long pull.
Having come into the world
through the gate between a woman's legs,
I want to know what it's like to want
above all to go back and back
to that early confinement in the dark.

I want to be a man,
to go where I want and when,
to earn a man's pay and then
to wonder, like a dog wonders
at the stove when the bacon
is frying, what it's like
to be such a strange, unlikely thing
as a woman.

Judith H. Montgomery

Service

My mother's ax rusts by the pump,
the shaft I tamped worn under sweat

and salt, grain blood-marked by blisters
split when she split the last stubborn

cord, glazed in late November sleet
that sheeted clod-hard ground and stump,

layering the shed until it slumped.
That shattered roof's now dried and bleached

in brilliant sun that glances from
black serge shined against smoothed pews,

threadbare lace of ironed handkerchiefs,
the parson's bald head sloped above

his book of prayer, its leather warped
by thumb and August's stiff corn heat.

The neighbor's cakes are cut inside.
I hunker here in straw-dried weeds

to test the blade, red as rust can
make it still sharp enough beneath

the flakes to split a thumb, a stack
of oak, a knotted, sap-sore heart.

Carly Sachs

Kent, Ohio

July 15, 2001

Nothing feels right for holding.
I dissolve into dusk's belly,
the hollow mouths of poems.
I've been taking long walks around this town,
not sure if I'm taking in or letting go.
I want to ask someone if this is transcendence
or if I can bum a cigarette.
If I could inhale you, I would ask you in,
bring you home. But I have no walls,
and my floor is water, then it is air.
The difference between drowning and breathing
is how fast you move your arms.

Angela D'Arista Solli

Diet Man

There's a belly in heaven that I love.
It wriggles with satisfaction
like a Buddha's would
at the sight of Jello and whipped cream.
    It doesn't give a damn.
There's a belly in heaven that I miss.
        It jiggles with beer.
It's great for a hug and a squeeze.
It devours cakes, cookies, and pies.
It shakes, rolls, and giggles at bad jokes.

        Get out of my sight diet man.
Take a hasty trolley to hell
            mean man,
            lean man,
            bean man,
            exacting man.

        Scram
new man,
reasoning man,
jogging man,
calculating man,

        whose thoughts you won't reveal,

sly man.

Elizabeth Whyman

Feedback as Requested

We devised, implemented and monitored
the project so acutely
we have surpassed all targets.

Because we organised and marketed ourselves
as part of an ideal package
and scheduled our selves to a deadline

Because our skills now lie more in
troubleshooting and problem-solving,
rather than the maintenance of relationships

Because we are team players
with an astute awareness of the field,
having researched the market well.

Because we no longer have time
to co-facilitate the discussion of our souls
I regret to inform you

That although you were an ideal candidate
the exchange is no longer reciprocal.
The deal is now closed, signed off.

Because our company strategies have changed,
I regret to inform you that your services
Are no longer required.

V. T. Abercrombie

The Great Blue Heron Is a...

Two blue herons, sentinels, unmoving,
on a high pine branch, observe us, me
on the glider, grandson, grandfather
putting large plastic sacks filled with
minnows and perch into the pond. Do
they calculate the distance the fish will
swim, the effect of sudden change, how
long it will take the minnows to find
the shallow shore, to be dinner? Blurred
in the crook of two limbs like my memories
of you, the twiggy nest holds the herons'
future. The splash of released water, ripples
of fish glinting like bits of broken glass,
the herons' deep raspy call, a flash of
wings, cloud shards of late-night regrets.

Cher Holt-Fortin

What The Dead Do

I've been saying goodbye for years.
So why won't you go?
You are dead.
And we'd been divorced for 12 years.
How is it you reappear,
uninvited, presumptuous, self-centered
as always,
content to show up in my mind's eye—
there, under those almond trees
where we rode our bikes on my 20th birthday,
in the Italian countryside;
or sliding up beside me
at traffic lights,
a phantom with your pale hair,
reddish beard, round face?

I'm sorry.
I'm tired of these ghostly visitations.
Go now.
Rest.
I forgive you.

Meg Petersen

My Debt to the Moon

When I was thirteen
I was drawn into step with the moon,
felt its pull
like the tide, like a wave
that swept away the world
I'd known, giving my body over
to heat.

Childhood is precious.
You don't know until,
with one glance of moonglow
through a window, or a transom hole
at just the right time,
you are caught and held fast
in the headlights of oncoming
puberty.

That was long ago.
I have made my peace with moon cycles
hardly noticed how they washed over me,
as I gave and gave and gave
my monthly tithe,
stopping only in pregnancy,
feeling the tides move within,
lapping up inside me.

So now the debt is paid,
and the moon would cast me off.
I skip a beat, and fall out of its rhythms.
They release me, leaving me
relieved yes, but oddly nostalgic
as it becomes
only a sliver, a crescent
waning.

Chris Waters

Empty Nest

The phone is almost mute. More than once,
his place was almost set; once it was, even.
For Elijah, their freshman fledgling flown off.

Minutes into the meal, he'd arrive glum. Persistence
had finally dislodged him from the monitor.
Turning dessert down, he'd rise. So much to do.
Especially those last weeks, his chums shooting off
one by one, expanding universe. Lucky the night
he was back by twelve. Back to the blue screen
(his parents are computer dorks) until, at two,
the footsteps up might awaken one parent or the other.

At least, no more guilt trips for asking asking asking
him to mow, take out the trash, bring empty glasses down.
Oh laziness contest won by the boy under the figtree—
supine, openmouthed, frozen—waiting for a fig
to fall just right. Oh pond goldfish, hovering
at the bottom, waiting for the flakes to swing down.

How many home runs? The futile stabs at common grounds.

His door is always wide open now, not pulled ajar
as it was after the late Instant Messenger times.
(What went on? Is he still doing it there?)
The porch lights go off now when they go up.
No more wet towels on the floor. Father's ties stay put.

His bed's made and crumbleless, no dirty socks underneath,
No Oreos, no only half-drunk cans of soda on the table.

It would be nice to recognize the house again.

Nancy Collins Boardman

Holidays

we are together this December
white pine
white chocolate
the fire is polite
coaxing frost from our sophistication

we prod memories from paper faces
in tattered albums
that recline like friends
on sunburned beaches

we remember more than we trade
in the surge and fatigue of flames
in the soft sizzle of boiling snow

Chella Courington

Blue

Judith drives a Peugeot
into my life of cheap jobs.

She tenders marriage of possibility
speaks of Greece and romance
the Caribbean and love

offers to share her house
built practicing the law.

Her proposal answers years
of my living on the edge.

I put on a wife's smock.
Judith would not see it the way a man does
in his own reflection.

She is not a renegade
would not break our vow
to shelter and warm each other.

Judith thumbs through cases of alimony
buries herself in briefs
hands me a list of honey-dos
before turning in.

She ransacks my closet
throws out clothes she doesn't like
screams at me when I mention school.
I forget to pick up her laundry.
She storms out and slams the door.

Like a nightingale who sings in darkness
I write till I'm weary
of a partner who fucks me blue.

Helen Marie Casey

On the Anniversary of Your Death

In the end, Emily, we are *all* alone,
living more in our mind
than anyone surmises.
We ravel thought,
transforming one idea
into its opposite, writing
our way for no one
so much as ourselves.
We must create to live.
The world longs
to be deciphered, or
is it the other way
around—we long
to decipher the world?
Finding the word
that works
becomes our passion,
appetites for solitude,
and books, insatiable.
We must craft
our own landscape the way
we piece a quilt, one tentative
seam after another,
endless variations
on death and possibility.
As for love, we find ourselves
listing, as if in the act of revision,
starting to say— then doubting—
what art can penetrate,
what mortals can divine.

Andrena Zawinski

I Am Reminded When Thinking

I am reminded, almost as if in whispers
by weathered house plaques on backstreets
of Prague, that behind the damp and musty
walls, those of some importance once must have

invented themselves above the rest of us here
who, ordinary, press our pens to pads,
our noses to fogged window panes to watch
and clock the melancholic morning drizzle.

Dustbins and brooms push in along the River
Vltva in a hush where shopkeepers drape doors
in lengths of amber beads jostling marionettes,
where sidewalk vendors fling open stall displays,

where I am reminded how shelves are stocked
in a new abundance with buxom breads, aged
cheese, pickled eggs and Postum. But how still now
the boat dock silenced of ragtime bandstands

and jazzy improvisational cafes, and how later dim
saloons will dance with consonant strung syllables,
how under doorways, in corridors, behind walls,
some of us will find each other with fingertips

and tongues, how we will

make promises and plans, interpret dreams, float
buoyant and rest on the wake of some small slice
of happiness, or on broken speech fill pillows
in relentless streams of muffled grief beneath

rime-colored skies the ravens cry. I am reminded
other mornings will wash in misty above sills,
a flurry of poppies in the rain-cleared air, halos
of canopies shading the light, reminded we are all

but ordinary mortals here taking on these uphill
cobbled paths where Kafka walked and stopped
above the long stretch of red rooftops to watch
how golden the charm of turrets and domes

held captive by this mother with claws,
how we can regret only that we are not birds.

Rhoda Janzen

The Shiverin' Bits

twilight and evening bell
—*Alfred, Lord Tennyson*

See what happens when you try
not to remember an advertising ditty,
try not to read the billboards placed by
some thoughtful editor in your pretty

margins. You're finally here on Lake Mac
kicking your feet to a distant boat's bell,
watching a pair of unfocused egrets attack
whatever lies under the water— or, hell,

maybe they're just grooming. The point is,
it's the shoreline, your beach, your neighbor
with the little-boy fountain taking a whiz,
the great reward of all your labor.

The chilled summer sky with its sweater
of clouds was just what you wanted:
the shiverin' bits as you opened your letter
from L.A. a woody house a little haunted

by a crusty gent in creased serge pants;
to wake up wondering why those tiny lights spin;
to see the water ruffled up with romance
unrelenting as a spicy harlequin.

It's like a dance with too much liquor—
the billboards roughly tap your shoulder,
so aggressive cutting in that you feel sicker,
such intoxicating vim that you feel older.

And it's not that you're a slow or dreamy dancer,
In the weird half-light the brashest billboards seem
altogether unaware of your new and tender cancer—
Prices Slashed, Jesus Rules, and Try Our Meat Supreme.

Kamilah Aisha Moon

Requiem for a Close Friend

Suddenly,
only a picture or an inside joke left
in the lost and found.
Suspended in the last act it drew breath—
fingers clutching a telephone,
a pen that makes a sharp detour down
a half-written page. Or lingering
as a hospice patient,
the occasional reflex confused
for revival.

Tonight,
I mourn the conch atop the bookcase.
Examining its shellacked, unnatural luster—
muscle scraped clean
like watermelon from the rind.
No more two-part harmony and fingers sticky
with wide-eyed love,

just blood roaring inside aging shell.

Lisa McMann

Dead Branches

You will know,
when the owl comes back to the dead branches
and he repeats the same familiar call
from midnight 'til one,

and you are able,
between the intervals,
to drift off in the comfort of his voice,

that tomorrow
the sorrow will be blanketed
by low murmurs of a settled coziness
hovering about the swaying hips
of white-dusted pines
and cones that twirl from red yarn.

Jessica G. de Koninck

The Poem I Did Not Write

I did not write the poem about getting
            hit by the car
because I did not need to get
            hit by a car

Not literally

The central metaphor of my life
            is accident enough

I hate everyone
            feeling sorry for me

All I wanted
when I got home
            from the ambulance
            and the ER
            and the pain medication
was a cup of hot tea and a hug

I can take care of myself
            but I don't want to
                        not on the day I get
            hit by a car

And I don't want
            a nurse
            mother
            friends

I want
            what everybody wants

Someone who loves me
            best in all the world

Someone I can call to say
    Don't worry
    I'm okay

I wish
    you did not die
I want
    you to come home

The driver said
    he never saw me

Christopher Woods

Woman with Fevers

All those years she lived
In that time-yellowed shack,
Windows opened wide in winter
And, come summer, fireflies
Roaming the rooms,
We never knew.

Even in desperate boyhood,
When the young toughs,
Our gonads all ablaze,
Stood, cheered and cajoled
In her worn dirt sideyard,
Singing, begging for her
To come out, all of us
Imagining her famous hot breath
Blowing across our thighs.
Not until she died
Did we have any idea
Why her body temperature
Always hovered at one hundred and four.
How her insides simmered,
If her dreams smoked
Even on frosted nights.
After the autopsy, the coroner,
Encouraged by too many beers,
Revealed what he found inside her.
Row after row of tiny suns,
Some large as pearls,
Each of them glistening,
Bestowing light and heat.

Maybe we were amazed. But in another week
We went back inside.
Ourselves, is what I mean.
Pretended we knew nothing
About the way she lived,
How well she had managed
With what was dealt her.
Perhaps she was better
Than the rest of us.
But if we felt this
We kept it to ourselves,
Locked in our cold hearts.
In time, we buried it
Beneath our ways.

Carly Sachs

Mourner's Kaddish, a Variation

it's not the death we mourn
because it's the death we carry
knowing only that part of the life we lose is our own

it is a collapsing of the soul like that of a star
and we fear we may forget

so we breathe life back into scented scarves, vacant mirrors
carry our dead in embroidered tablecloths, costume jewelry,
our own names.

Jeremy Farrington

Doorway

I'm sitting in my car
outside your house
late in the afternoon,
the snow banks alongside the road dark from exhaust.
I stare at your door, not sure whether you are home or not,
although I have a feeling you are.
I think about knocking
imagining your face as you open the door,
the kind of surprise that would register
from not seeing me in four years,
a smile and a hug.
What keeps me in the car is the thought that
perhaps you wouldn't smile,
maybe slap me for losing touch
or worse maybe you wouldn't remember me at all.
I never explained
why I drifted away from you then
and don't think that I could now either.
Out of the corner of my eye, I notice
the clock on the dash change,
put the car in drive
and leave.

Barbara Schweitzer

The Spendthrift Heart

Heartache
leaks in slowly.
A burst is always too fatal.
The veins practice their collapse
in even steps like tiny gasps
that come up finally empty of air.
You tell me you cannot be there
when future scratches at our door.
Not in death, you take yourself away.
Not in despair. Not even in the
absence of heat. But in
abstemious retreat from
my spendthrift heart.
You withdraw where
I invest, even with
your penurious
interest.

Audrey Friedman

On Algebra Test Mornings

the fragrance of your White Shoulders
whispered to me all day as I stroked
the white rabbit's foot keychain
you had slipped into my trembling hand.

The fur was already rubbed
to near-baldness. If only I could go
back to when I was in love with you,
mother, when you smiled and said

Kiss the mezuzah on the way out
the door for luck. And for insurance,
make sure to step over the threshold
with your right foot first.

V.T. Abercrombie

The Shell Game

Like a duffle bag, loosely packed,
just this side of worn out, you
appear on my doorstep. *Yes?*
I say. You give a little wave.
With a con man's smile and sleight
of hand you shift the walnut shells
again the way a tattered beard,
ancient eyes can hide the misplaced
child I finally recognize. Your
clothes. You say you want them.
In your arms my hopes, folded
between useless garments,
travel with you to the street,
discarded like yesterday's promise.

Laurence J. Sasso Jr.

Father's Mission

Somewhere in the sun-welded weeds
father's pliers lie,
rusted to a caked oxide
as unrecognizable as he is
Never stopped looking
for them, even when
his breath came in gulps
and he took a limb to walk
Out there where alders
are overtaking the orchard
and brambles lock the paths
he went each night while it was light
Poking at the grass and thickets
his foot sucked down by marshy ground
he was certain he could find them,
perfect for the small jobs, the hard places
Mother worried at the hour
and the strain, hoped the dogs
stayed with him, gripped by this thing
so treasured he couldn't let it go

Elizabeth Thomas

Seventeen

I knew you once—
long, straight hair parted down the middle,
thin arms, olive skin,
mottled bruises
hidden beneath your favorite shirt

and the little boy
whose hands you loosely hold
to help him stand.
He tilts to one side
unsure of his footing,
but holds his head high
and looks directly at me.
You look down,
away from the eyes that appraise you,
away from the eye of the camera.

I see you have tried
to make the room cozy—
cinder block shelves,
a record player
though no records lean beside it,
a donkey the size of your son
won by your father
when you were nine,
a child's plastic pool, a plant

and on the wall behind you,
a watercolor of ocean and sky
painted by an old man
from the coffee shop
to make you smile.

At forty-three
there is not much I wouldn't do
to know what you were thinking
when this picture was taken—
to meet you again,
hold your hands,
watch your head lift high.

Lisa McMann

Churn

Musky fragrance sprained,
twisted through thinning creases in
parched cracked walls.

Choices chip opaque film
exposed, regretted.

Closed wounds burst inside,
cluster, blister, churn.

Suzanne Sigafoos

Delia D., 1970

Convinced her cowgirl boots are haunted, she keeps
them at a distance from her *huaraches* and her red high-tops,
secures the boots in a turquoise Samsonite Overnighter locked
tight and stashed in shadow, the tiny key on a black string
around her neck. She fears the perpetual night that lives

inside her Escher-patterned, black & white movie star boots,
cannot trash them, can't resist trotting them out
for high rock n' holy roll times and I mean high,
like when The Stones play The Garden. First class airfare,
suite at the Plaza, a couple lines of coke and only then can she

insist her toes, arches and ankles into the sinister leather.
Dark hair starred with gardenias, slinky red dress, she is all
style and prance, arms raised so the songs can enter her, dancing in
the aisle inside music loud as a steel mill. Back in Ohio,
she pounds on my door at three in the morning, tells me

if only she hadn't worn the goddam bad vibe boots,
of course Mick would have seen her moves in her new red dress,
of course Mick would have fucked her, tells me over and over,
chanting and pacing, her pupils black moons,
dawn locked away in the dark.

Kathryn Kulpa

Bed Cats

for Ruth Bailey

One is long, deep-chested, wide
of eye, with lion's gait;
Big cat paws knead pillow, arm,
or breast until he finds his place.

One is monkey-tailed, snake-headed,
shy of voice, with Roman nose;
She purrs at first touch, stretches, shows
her spotted belly, rolls.

Soft cats live in winter beds.
I have waked with fur-capped head,
their dreams pressed against my spine.

Do they dream of arms
that held them? Do they mourn?
Do cats know time?

Outside the sounds of ducks and geese,
in some far harbor a ship's horn.
They speak of flight.
I dream of loss

But bed cats dream themselves a home.

Anna Claire

I adore Anna Claire.
She has soft brown hair, deeply violet eyes.
I ask Jesus to make mine just like hers.

We seal a pact in blood—
best friends forever—
prick our index fingers,
press them so tight
the tips turn white.

September we bury photos
taken in a booth where we played hooky.
We grin, hug, kiss, and wave.

We share Saturday night basement parties.
Mostly girls dance with girls
but some boys, like Billy Frank, break in.

Anna Claire calls him a clod with two left feet.
When he walks away to put on Johnny Mathis,
she grabs my hand, drags me to the side.
'Chances Are' is our song.

He calls Anna Claire *a downright bitch,*
sometimes to her face, more often to mine.
He usually sounds full of himself
like the time he asks me to the drive-in,
says I better go or he'll nab a real girl.
Anna Claire laughs,
ugly jackass.

He's okay, not a dreamy Troy Donahue
but other girls want him.
I don't turn him down.
Anna Claire flies into me,
says not to do anything I don't want to.
You're just a yellow-bellied sapsucker.

She's right.
I want to dance, sing, talk away the days with her.
At fourteen I desert Anna Claire,
move to another world
where real girls do exactly as they want.

Jeremy Farrington

Birthday Party

Friday night, I tried
to use spirits to scare you from my head,
but only woke Saturday
to thoughts of you, a hangover
and a mouth too dry to admit
that maybe I had been wrong.

Sometime while I was out,
I switched from Canadian whiskey to Irish
hoping that the taste might mimic that of your lips.
While the liquid burned like you,
it tasted far too earthy for your stellar body
around which I used to orbit.

The bartender asked what I wanted.
Knowing you weren't on the menu, I ordered beer.
I thought about how your hair looked blonder than the beer did,
except at the roots and noticed that the blue on the label was close
enough to make me think of your eyes. I haven't seen them
since past this beer's *Born on Date*, although it seems much longer.

The bartender walked over with a slab of cake on a plate,
the candle stuck in it looked as drunk as I did,
leaning to its left and lit. Placing it in front of me he said,
Make a wish. I thought of you and how I missed you,
watched the candle fall off the top of the cake
and felt the burn on my fingers when I tried to catch it.

Pat Hegnauer

Last Words

I'm going to my grave with a strangle
of words, taking unsaid love like sour
cud to ferment in the muddy tangle
of roots, stones, and my long entrenched hours.
I've stored away unaccomplished passion
and undeclared lust in closet boxes,
left dreams on cold shelves to die of famine,
and eliminated foolish flashes
that tempted me to write an honest page.
I bequeath our dumb mediocrity
to the loud but speechless children. Assuage
them with bonds and Wall Street security
instead of chapters from my maudlin heart
whose poetry might make it hard to part.

Elizabeth Scism

Ocean Isle Beach, 1964

—for Hampton, who later ran for help...

Moments earlier you sat inside the cool mouth
of our tunnel, just a boy bent over sand dollar fragments—
When they're whole, you grinned,
you can shake'em and hear small doves inside...

Doves.
A child's myth for a child—
beating against thin shell like small bones, those wings.
Your death must have been like that: beautiful, grotesque—
the sharp, thin blades of your shoulders
folding in, folding in...

But as the tunnel walls caved in on your bones
and your shells, I stood yards away by the shore.
While your slim body curved between the teeth
of our tunnel, I stood mesmerized by minnows
that shimmer in shallow waters.

Margo Solod

I Still Have Everything You Gave Me

Though I lost your wedding ring, I might
have left it in the rental house in Lexington
or maybe on a train.
I lost the gold chain
that you gave me too, in Michigan
Beth took it off on our last night
and I forgot to put it on again.

I think the rug you gave me's still
boxed up in Jay's attic
if he hasn't given it
away, I'm sure the metal
dog and wooden horse are safe, I left them

on the island with your mother's silver,
her good dishes and her serving trays
as well as all the macramé you tied.
The bonsai died
But I still have the pot somewhere.
If what they say
is true and all your body's cells change over

every seven years, well, I'm forty-two
and there is nothing I can do to change that,
but I swear no matter what I lose
I still have everything you
gave me, I carry it inside, curled tight
a fist I'm too afraid to open, too afraid I'll use.

Lawrence Schimel

Fairy Tales for Writers: Sleeping Beauty

There are many who yearn to be frozen
while their youth is at its peak,
to stretch out that ephemeral time
into a hundred years or more.

There are others who seem not to discover themselves
until late in life, following sundry other paths
until they stumble upon a true vocation, such as writing.
We call them sleeping beauties, these authors
who blossom in a later season, their measured, mature prose
a welcome antidote to the youthful brouhaha
that's all the rage in the marketplace these days.

But far too many are the true sleeping beauties,
who at a tender age find a harsh critic
who berates their talent and their fantasies
with a verbal barb sharper than the nib of any fountain pen
that silences the stories, poems, daydreams
they might have written.

Be it from parent or teacher, sibling or spouse,
just one tiny prick of criticism is all it takes sometimes
to put a burgeoning writer to sleep
for a hundred years,
for a lifetime,
for so long that no princes are left
to hack through the brambles,
or if one is, he can't imagine that he should bother.

Suzanne Sigafoos

Despite Cancer and the Ohio Winter Mother Insists I Drive Her to Visit Lila's New Baby

Weak as a string but able to hold a newborn on her lap
this visit is close to over according to me her eldest
daughter back in town to lend a hand, smarting
from the latest love gone wrong and shocked to see
Mother faded, but this day her voice is strong if not oracular.
Declaring the baby girl beautiful, she sees a bright future
for Lila's first child. Lila-who-married-well reclaims her daughter

invites us upstairs to see the nursery. Mother ascends laughing
and talking like footage from another decade stands three seconds
in the cheerful room I cannot stop the falling she reaches for me
down we go. A peripheral ballet: Lila on the phone her husband the
EMT's then Dad all dashing past me dazed and sitting on the stairs
up to the nursery where Mother's out cold. Stretcher.

Siren. No, they tell me, go back to the house. The ice.
The car fishtails once or twice but it's OK—I steer
into the skid. At the house a letter no word
from this old lover in years no hello no how are you
no news or small talk a letter that begins with how the sex
was how his hands remember. I feel faint. The phone

Dad' voice: she's conscious now they want to keep her
overnight she got a private room this time what's for supper
then he's home and Guido our old boxer whimpers
stumbles it's his heart Dad says carrying blankets downstairs
so he won't be alone, lies on the couch, one arm over the edge
his hand on Guido's broad chest the dog on the soft rug
dreaming legs moving broken hearts everywhere.

Andrena Zawinski

Note from a Motel

And here I am again, alone again, somewhere rainy
off an Interstate connection, bleary-eyed and weary,
hopscotching map lines figuring how to get back,
back to you. I've held on to the note you slipped me,
a ticket out, heavy-handed as a stone cutter's
epitaph in granite: I've had it, it's too much,
        this is where it all stops.

And I know it's not the end
of the world, even in this loneliness the panic of No
Vacancy signs along the dark and rain soaked coast
I've roamed. But here, the quiet
        could be deadly.

Do you know what I mean? Can you possibly
get this? I could become some woman in a dim lit bar,
hiking up her skirt in an urgency for love.
Could you forgive that? Have you
        heard this before?

        But things could be worse. I could bump around
        outside up against the muggy midnight sky, weepy
        for you. By the time this gets to you, there could be
        a tidal wave, cars might crash, ships wreck, a star
        burn out. And we will have had this accident
        of time apart to sleep and dream and think.

        Yet I do nothing but dread our days cut short.
        You don't believe me? Here's the key.
        Let your senses bring you to me. Drag your bags in
        here across the floor. The earth might move.
        We could really make some noise.

Elizabeth Whyman

Jeans

I've had more wear out of these jeans
than I've had out of my father.

They've been twenty years consistent,
and three whole daughters strong.

When I chased a burglar out the house
it was these I pulled on first.

Comforting, that they've suited so long
and never tired or worn out.

After all these years, it's fitting,
that all I have of him are these jeans.

Michele F. Cooper

Mission

Brown hawk in her dark fall tweeds
makes a third pass over the

immemorial marshes and earth
lands east of the beach,

doesn't understand why she can't
find the waves of grass and reeds,

the browns, then greens, then browns
again as the years cycle from daisies

to rose hips, goldenrod to bittersweet
on the sandy borders of home.

It isn't possible to digest the barren
flats, brown earth naked in the sun,

open to the moon's total eclipse
but closed to her hunt.

She circles, sweeps across the acres
high and low, flapping her spotted

arms, frowning under the close
feathers on her head and neck.

She is angry, riled at the loss,
would fall apart at the offense

to generations, the broken code,
except that somewhere she can't

locate yet, her last chick still
shivers in the pond grass where

he somehow fell in their escape
from the tractors and sledges.

A sixth pass now,
a seventh.

Joyce Sakala

List

I regret stepping in that
puddle, walking on the pier and
staring at the sea
until I made that one mistake,
and my sneaker filled with the
shock of cold water

I regret not getting in that boat with that
man as he cruised away from the yacht club
dock effortlessly, alone

I regret not shouting and waving my arms,
running till my breath came in hard gasps
to call out
take me, take me

And I regret not falling off the edge of the pier into
the water, not floating face down in the shallows
able to see starfish and an old sunken
bicycle
I regret staying
dry

I regret careful steps, careless steps, steps not taken
and steps in the wrong direction
I regret these steps that carry me uphill
home
inside
warm
safe
alone.

Louis E. Bourgeois

Of the Liquid Trees

...And I grow weaker, weaker every day
having forced too much upon the world,
having forced pen to paper...
And the penalty is that I have
lived too long...
I am a coward, a comic martyr,
who has stayed on the
stage too long, far too long
and there is nothing left to do...
I fool myself into thinking
it was all an illusion that it all
didn't matter, and, of course, it
matters, everything matters, it's
all a game, a role, chosen
by some inquisitor, we will
never know, and nothing
is too bright and dark
and nothing sinks like mud
and nothing is my god, and it's
all Donna... Nothing itself is changing me...

Cecelia Hagen

Raccoon

I understand you more or less
lost all respect for me
when I didn't understand
that raccoon metaphor
in the poem you sent.

But because we're good friends you haven't
said as much to me. The weight of it
visits me at vulnerable times—
when I'm making up the twin beds
or pumping gas in some other state. I'm dense

in my own cocoon, you probably
know that too well.
What you don't see, in my opinion, is your own
mummy bag, the way it cramps your style. Wait,
there's that raccoon again. Let's see

if I can get him this time, snugged
into one of my expertly tucked hospital corners
or swooning in the fumes of my topped-off tank.
No, he's gone, his improbable tail
following the wake of his walk

like a lie detector follows a lie. They say it takes
two people to make the truth,
one to say it and one to hear. You,
could you take a moment
and make this true?

N.M. Brewka

Broker

He blows in begging on a March blizzard,
the original fair-haired boy who poisoned himself
with bad alchemy, a strung-out harbinger of
hell's spring groaning up the driveway in his
broken-down Chevy to knock at the door and
sell himself once more with a sly humility.
He's checked himself out of the private asylum
where a born-again client had insisted on footing
the bills to raise him from the wreckage of his
Wall Street minerals firm, gold stock blown to
angel dust. When I tell him my mother, his aunt,
had died and been buried back in February,
he sits, candy belly bulging, staring that ward stare.

Outside, wearing a loose, brownish kimono—
God knows what institutional laundry spawned it—
and boat shoes with rawhide laces untied, his thighs
fat as a jolly friar's or a murderous Henry the Eighth's,
he smokes unfiltered Camels behind the wheel,
radio on and door open while we boil his clothes.
At night, the stairs creak. Our whole bodies cock
for the surreptitious slide of the knife drawer, lunatic
rummage among mouse turds and twist-ties.
The bathroom door opens and closes, opens again.
We don't grow used to this, even though it proves
time after time after time after time that he hasn't
come to kill us but to favor us with his need.

It snows. It snows again, harder. Outside, he shifts
behind the wheel and smoke pours out into the world
from his mouth like a terrible idea. In his fantasy,
he's still rich, owns us all, owns the world, the roads,
the churches, the towers, the mines and the caves
where, like Ali Baba, he first met the thieves. At night,
the phone calls monitor the madness of a man who
won't work if he can't steal by peddling nothing real.

On his birthday, we have a cake, and a fight.
There's no money here, no sanctity, no solicitude,
only grief like a hangover, rage for the end of things.

Lin Nulman

Letter from the Shore

I. Halfway

By now you have a blizzard.
I guess I won't miss the time
spent digging out. It puts an end to autumn,
the endless jettison of leaves
down from the mountains. An orange one,
a red one, a yellow one, an
orange one, a red one, a yellow one
with orange, red with yellow, wet shreds
on both the cars, wadded dams in all the gutters,
dead crusts in the newspapers,
magazines, piles of mail, leaves blowing
through the front door, back door,
in the wake of your boots, mixing with
everything. Yesterday you bought
a second rake, to lean in line
with your pair of shiny shovels.
Today I left.

II. There

My room is pale green, the old quilt an indigo
so deep, it disappears at night.
Every day I get two towels:
hands and body. I have a table,
paper, a pen, an armchair
beneath a charcoal drawing of one ship.
A white buoy on a shelf holds up a book
about the birds to be seen here.
They don't live in trees. Each morning
I find small drifts of sand on the windowsill
that are gone with a breath.

The sharp calligraphy of dune grass
bends in the wind above the wild peas,
driftwood graying in the sun,
the purple shells that rest in place
like stars and fade into the tide. The ocean
makes up more than half of everything.
It swallows snow, crumbles the light
to be brushed away like dust.
It changes color by the hour, shades of blue
I might easily later forget,
or that might go unseen while I am
writing. Perhaps to someone.
A letter from here.

Helen Marie Casey

Absent

You ask me what I used to have, and love,
no longer have, and miss. All the while you know,
what it is I'm bound to say, though
neither of us wants it said. It's you I lack, you I miss.
You stand here, absent, even to yourself,
a thing mysterious as it is sad. If there were
ways to put you back together, more whole
than you have ever been, I would begin
the soldering but I cannot, cannot find the way
to know, do you want to be whole or is there
something dark you've learned to love
and cannot do without, something almost tangible
you long to put your arms around, to claim as better
than it was before, when all was Ivory bright?

Barbara Schweitzer

Thinsulated

We harvest them from their rooftop garden,
saw-tooth denizens of deep winter, jagged
     ice teeth that seem from the warm inside to chew
the tangle of pine before our cooler
     swallows them down,
cold packs for the sturgeon and
     champagne you have brought to celebrate
my return.

     My heart is their metaphor:
     I am half-here, re-measuring the fraction, dear,
meting out my recovery from our distance.

     Your hope is downy comfort, feathering my pulse
but I feel your thrust like a wild mink that must
     not ferret for the warm parts,
must remain the casual underside of the thrush,
     careful not to break the germs we've just
entrusted to the nest.

     (We are on black ice still,
     not out of the Black Forest yet, not out of
the pitch of night, the tar pit of mis-sayings.
     Don't cinch us in your Ulster yet.)

     Let us bring out the caviar, black eggs
we will fertilize with our acid tongues, eggs once
     with as much future as June weddings,
gutted and spilled in the blue dish you
     did not forget.

     You wipe the tulip Waterfords. Your smile
     could unfreeze that whole row of icicles
we left hanging, the fringe of dusk
     eking in our window.

"It must be cold," you say, some temperature,
you say, it must be chilled to some
temperature for its peak flavor,
some number, like ten years together,
some number I could forget, too, as you twirl,
twirl, and twirl the black bottle in the
silver bucket.

Your smile, your long fingers twitching for me,
contain themselves over the crystal
glass you hold out to me—

your smile, your eyes, grasping, aching;
no words can undo your eagerness.
You are home, you think, have fastened up the dogs,
put away the sled, you are crawling
inside our thinsulated bag, zip up the container;
you have wrapped me up again,
and yes,

you are too happy as I take the glass and
swallow hard, unleashing hot tears.
"It's the champagne," I say.

"Too cold?" you ask.

Invitation #2

Come to me.
Be one with my absurdities.
The mountain quivers in the gunmetal heat
And what voices I thought I longed for
Babble in a pencil case. Come, I say.
Don't just stand there like an end table
Polished stupid. I don't give a swipe
For all your on-guard sensibilities.
Watch my mouth. I am not your wallpaper.
I am not your Channel 8. The owl's swoop,
The mouse's cry, play out against dusk's
Well-oiled machinery. Even the colors
Fall into disrepair. We are not exempt.
The time devoted to writing this
Could have been heaven in a hammock
Kissing the no out of your mouth.

Shulla Sannella

Regret

for Robert L. Smith, poet emeritus

A mutual friend calls
to tell me of your death
last night in New York.
I find your poems.

It pains me that I will
never see your face again
and that when I left you
on that hot rainy evening
it was adieu.
I would have stayed so much longer.

I would have brought you
two pounds of chocolate and
told you right then
when you handed me
your latest lines
how true your writing was.

You reiterate that I will continue
guarantee it is never over
and that if you risk life and love
some marvel will most certainly
smite you across the heart
and drive you to language.

As if your death could not
bring me to that door
that opens on the sadness
and the absence of one who loved me.

Pat Hegnauer

Deus ex Machina

I am the deus ex machina,
the palpable shadow
dogging the striding him,
the smoldering him,
and the graying him,
the plump arms that open
obedient as an elevator door,
the ride to the penthouse,
breakfast in bed,
sun on the balcony.

I am the unplanned solution,
the late-night listener,
red psychiatrist couch,
the lake that hides the lady,
tongue that licks wounds
and bandages with words,
the map used on the journey,
maiden praying at home.

I am the vague reminder,
the dream in a yellow dress,
confusing perfume from a flower,
the exotically set table,
candle swallowing the dark,
music shifting behind duty,
a tune that hides for days
then jumps into his hum.

Teresa Joy Kramer

Cherubs

Your daddy mailed you angels,
white plaster of Paris, to guard
and keep you, he'd say each time,
each year as it fell away.

Last fall you brought them all upstairs,
a gift to me, you said, arranging all
six in a curve like an "S" —a man-made
snake—across my dresser, right
in front of the newly framed photo
of me at my second wedding.

I have let them stay as you placed them
and ask no questions of you,
like why some of them touch,
why others don't, why the "S."

Each morning I wake earlier
than the rest of this house in the making.
I stand, I reach, and I open
the drawers of the dresser I once shared
with your father.
With each drawer I close, the hulky piece
shakes, rattling the ceramic clutter
of crowded angels, wings
plastered to their sides.

Suzy Lamson

2 A.M.

It's late
The ghosts of unsent letters haunt me:

The unwritten condolence note
for that iron-willed wisp of a woman
whose death left a husband bereft,
left to gnaw upon fifty years' memories
flavored salty by the future;

last week's half-finished answer
to a loyal friend's chatty letter
stands like a lone palm silhouetted
dark and solitary against a tropic sunset.

The constellations move across the sky's horizon
while my thoughts scratch futilely
like half-started poems or unsaid retorts
for offenses whose well-deserved rejoinders
never reached audibility.

It's late and night is a time for conscience—
firefly thoughts lighting the darkness
while I toss under heavy sheets of obligation and guilt.

Catherine McCrane Keating

A Journey from Rhode Island to Florida

Detour signs ahead ~
In the Fall of my trip
I've lost my roadmap.

My Bay's abandoned ~
Exchanged for blank white beaches
And bland Southern drawls.

Having an Ocean ~
How can I regret a small
Salt-water Bay?

From my porch I saw
Flotillas of sloops, geese, swans ~
Not a wooden fence.

At dawn on the beach,
My love and I kissed and held ~
Our old age at bay.

It's clear to me now,
I came to walk winter beaches ~
And let in the sunrise.

Davi Walders

Requiem for Judith Resnick

"The world looks great." —J. R. from the space shuttle Discovery, 1984

Sometimes as though you were hovering,
as though you wished someone—anyone

to remember, I see you, a young girl
polishing her shoes, packing her lunch,

concentrating and deliberate, each choice
as serious as the dinner discussions,

Torah portion and algebra equations
that challenged you. Granddaughter

of a shochet, connected to ritual, family
and community, I see you, not here

on Bethesda streets walking among us
during your long years of preparation,

but far away, as in those one hundred
forty hours floating beyond the pull

of gravity or in dim, humming rooms,
just above charts and graphs, searching

green screens for red warning lights.
Pilot of your own fearless trajectory,

always the first to arrive, to board,
you are the first to settle into that

locked weightlessness, rising again
those last moments of lift-off, given

neither wings, nor chariot, nor chance
to fly too near the sun, leaving us

only the grace of a woman doing her
job and the dignity of your name,

that, too, eclipsed by others.

Ada Jill Schneider

Looking Backward

I haven't seen the other me
in a while. You know—
that woman trying
to build an umbrella
as large as the United States
to cover us all in case of rain.
She was the handle
holding the spokes
at eye level.
I do miss her.

When her high hopes
for world peace failed,
she retreated
to the last row of the
local Historical Society.
Her strident letters to editors
dissolved into minutes
for the Garden Club.
I grieved with her for years.

So I'm not the person
I set out to be.
When I wasn't looking,
I narrowed my focus
to family and people I meet.
Now I spread tolerance quietly
and carry a plastic rain bonnet
no one under sixty owns.
It doesn't poke anyone
in the eye and I'm prepared
for all kinds of weather.

Ruth Bailey

Ali, Short for Alexandra

You might think of Ali as a little girl whose wild gold curls drew pats from strangers at the grocery store in church on the street walking with her mother tall and dark and striking in herself but Ali follows Fransson the old Swedish woman who sweeps the street where Ali lives the leaves in the fall the dust in the Rhode Island summer and Ali follows her all the time listing to the right as Fransson does Ali the little gosling following this mother goose on her mother's busy frantic days trying to work and care for the new baby and not enough time but it's okay because Fransson sweeps the street and then feeds the cats the thirty cats or so all different colors and designs who eat from an old split pipe even when Fransson has no money for heat she has enough for cat food and Ali helps and Ali grows and soon plays in the street alone and goes away to school riding the short way to Wyman and then walking the long way to Aldrich and then to Pilgrim marking the changes from elementary to junior high to high school in Warwick which is the city where she lives and then her chubby beauty turns to long legs and darker hair and she goes away to college and then to work one summer in one of those Nevada towns to make enough for school and then this car let loose not on purpose but some weird accident this car climbs the sidewalk and Ali flies through the air and breaks the windshield and the ambulance comes and her father comes and her mother and her sister and her brother but she has nothing to say nothing to say for many days and her friends come from California and Rhode Island and Massachusetts and everywhere and phone calls are everywhere and Ali they tell her and did you know that this happened and that happened and here we are Ali and Ali has nothing to say but then one day her finger moves and then in some kind of unbelievable way she wakes and sometimes she hits her friends and they learn to be careful because the doctors say that happens to people with brain injuries and that's what happened her brain was injured but then she got better and then she went to school and to graduate school and now she's in love and maybe she'll get married and her brain doesn't hurt and who can tell in this life what happens next

James Cihlar

Expedition

Without being ponderous,
the cracked cookie jar's tag
announces $24.95, "as is."
Cream clapboard body, teal roof lid
with worn burgundy chimney pull.

I didn't want to write this poem,
but a taste of yours made me.
This weekend my blue Corolla took me
to the other side of the river,
a ring of thrift stores,

my old neighborhood,
to sift through the wreckage
of unknown neighbors' past lives,
seeking a glimpse of something simple,
plain objects forgotten and shared,

a flash to expedite insight into ten years ago,
the beginning of a long run of jobs,
unexpected bends in the road.
You say wanderlust is in the blood.
I could stop writing now, but I won't.

How long? Ten minutes, maybe,
staring at the thing is enough to tell me
I'd never be satisfied with this fractured jar,
its bad home repair work.
Instead, this trek delivers

yellow bamboo ceramic planter
that the collector's guide says is from 1974,
Schroeder and Lucy Welch's grape jelly jar,
a gift to match the one you bought this summer
two blocks from your mother's house,

a plate of the make my prodigal sister
collected back when she was anchored
in the deep blue front bedroom of home.
A flower vase in the shape of a woman's head,
cardinal perched on mod hat abover her enigmatic face.

Shelley Ann Wake

Can Anyone Spell "Indecision"?

Put your hand up, little girl.
You know the answer.
You can do it.

But no.
The word tumbles through your mind
and the letters jumble.
The slowly rising hand
creeps back down
to safety.

Then, "No!"
It's a loud voice,
a commanding voice.

"No," it says again.
"Don't put that hand down,
put that hand up proudly."

"Yes," it says.
It's quieter this time
but it sounds more like you.
Just a braver you.

The hand rises up into the air.
You want to punch it up into the air
but something slows it.
It's still rising though.
Casually,
but definitely,
rising.

Then she speaks.
"Yes, Daniel."
"I-N-D-E-C-I-S-I-O-N," says Daniel.
"Good," says the teacher.
"And a hard word too,
very good."

The hand flops down and lies at your side,
hanging there like a lifeless creature,
defeated.

"I knew that," another voice whispers.
You want to shout that out.
I knew that.
I knew that.
I knew that.

But the class has already moved on
to the next question.
"Can anyone spell regret?"

An easy one.
You could spell it.
But you can't now.
Too busy thinking
about indecision.

Susan Firghil Park

The End of the Daughters of Minyas

(after Ovid)

We refused to call him Son of Thunder, the Twice-Born,
the Deliverer, shunned his frenzy—pandemonium

of drums and horns, timbrels, fierce-haired
women shrieking, stampeding in wild dance—

for our quiet room of looms, choosing to weave
instead threads of old stories. For our sin Bacchus

morphed us into bats—our hands and thin arms shrank, grew
taut skin stretched to narrow ribs, shoulder blades

sharpened into lift of ridged, folding wings. Now we flit
at dusk, as other humans settle into our once-dear

households—just outside of lamplight, we skim
eaves and rafters, our story only told as high notes

carried off by the wind. We are the ghosts of regrets
surrounding you, flickers of shadows circling

between you and the faltering flame, just before
you bend near to blow it out for the night.

Kathleen Kirk

The Drawer

Her skin is gray with the dust of packing when
we come to take away the desk. Open
boxes strew the foyer like slit stomachs.
A lamp cord trails from one, a stray umbilical.
Her son is out riding his bike. The head of a bear
lolls on the floor of his room, plastic fangs
bared in rebuke. We turn away to the hamster,
curled against us, almost invisible
in its cave of sweet wood shavings. The cat,
dying, flickers down the narrow hall.
Susan guides us out the back door, to the yard:
the desk sits in the grass at the slight slant,
sprayed clean with the hose now flooding a bed
of impatiens—polished and angled in the round
profusion of peonies opened wide by the ants
still peeling back the newest buds, immobile
in the barely swaying still of afternoon.
One last bough of bleeding heart drips its pink
petals to earth. Scarlet columbine bends
in the pregnant air, trembling to see us go.
She shows us how the desk is small compared
to her son, who returns, tossing his bike aside.
She shows us how the drawer won't close, it sticks
in the humid air, she has to grip it tight,
but it won't be forced, she lets it jut out
like a jaw set against her world of regret
and when she suddenly weeps, we see the gift
for what it is, wide open.

Ruth Mark

This Time Will Not Come Again

Today I look out the window
revel in the delft blue sky.
This mundane Sunday
has disappeared like so much
rain in the ever-flowing river—
life coursing ever-onward
days melding into each other,
nights stacking their heads
one against the other against the other.
Will I rejoice in this time,
this monotony? They say
"no news is good news"
yet the endless anticipation
for something, anything
change comes quickly
or not at all. Perhaps I
have to make change
orchestrate my own symphony
I can not wait any longer.
This time has gone, it
will not come again.

Valerie Russo

The Rich Historian

I once believed in salvaging used things.
Items rich in history and experience,
still carrying the weight of someone's emotional manifestations.
Heavy engravings, markers of some past life,
deeply etched like synthetic veins on some inanimate object.
I once saw beauty in that pain.
That rawness that seeped out.
The tragedy which had transpired.
Speaking volumes on humanity.
The abandonment made richer the victim.
The neglect, part of the glory.
The bounty, mine. Or is it?
Like an isolated museum hall
do I not celebrate something
which is long gone. Encased in glass.
Extinct, no longer here, only a remnant
of what once was, an outer shell.
An eaten peanut, the seed of a mango
with all the juice sucked dry by another.
The empty chrysalis of April's butterfly in December.
What is it I once believed in?
Collecting things half gone, forgotten,
put aside, broken and dispossessed.
Wading through wreckage
to find that bounty that treasure to deify.
To idealize and identify.
To give a home to, still searching to heal the world.
No longer enough satisfaction in
just stray kittens but now shattered men to heal and mend.
Make shiny and new like that found penny or pearl button.
Found and lost.
Content with the load in my small pocket
or yesterday's little dirty fist of seashells,
and pretty stone, like that glittery one
at the beach or the downy feather,

or the fallen eyelash rescued from your cheek
and some confetti that descended
from your curls tight in my grip.
I once found comfort in my miniature menagerie
of odd artifacts. Odds and ends.
The salvaged and the wrecked, the chipped and the flawed,
the old and the timeless, misbegotten and misplaced.
Growing sedentary, I tire.
The weight of my altruistic meandering
growing obtrusive, getting the better of me.
As the day grows old, my dirty fists
wracked with pain, dirt and blood,
I wonder who will salvage me?

Barbara Crooker

Saying Goodbye

Apparently trivial detail. . . can show us the world, the beauty to
which we are always, sooner or later, saying good-bye.—Robert Kelly

October, and the late afternoon sun slants in,
laying down a glaze of gold from the west.
It's time to cut basil, snip and strip
the dark green leaves with their breath
of anise for pesto on a winter night,
when the sky is a lid of polished glass.

It's time to dry oregano, thyme, mint,
to simmer apples and cinnamon, mill them
down to sauce, a rosy reduction.

All summer, I've put up jars of jam:
raspberry, blueberry, blackberry, peach.
They sit smugly in the cellar
like money in the bank, their lids sealed
with such sweet certainty.

One night, a year from now, or twenty, or ten,
one side of this brass bed will be empty, one
pillow undented, one space under the log cabin
quilt smooth as stone. Sooner, or later, one of us
will sleep alone. And all these nights, katydids
arguing their did-nots/did-toos outside the screen,
when sleep takes us before love does, will be long
and black and full of regret.

Kake Huck

At Last Safe Harbor

The only time I visited your home
you showed me April grapes. Small bitter rounds
of promise cooled my palm. Caressing loam
you bragged of harvests born in potent mounds
of your design. Inside your house the shine
of hands on metal, wood, and paper proved
a life seduced by work kept happy time
as boundaries marked you husband, father, loved.

And yet as we talked shop your voice dropped low
and thickened like a woman's secret flower.
You closed your eyes. Your body stilled. I know
we could have shattered lives within that hour.

But ten years after, friend, I don't regret
I didn't weed the gardener from his bed.

Contributors

V.T. Abercrombie received the Book of the Year 2001 for Poetry award from the North Carolina High Country Writers Association for her book *Greatest Hits 1980-2000* published by Pudding House Press. Her poems have appeared in literary magazines such as *Roanoke Review, White Rock Review, Honey, Visions International* and several anthologies.

Ruth Bailey grew up in Waterbury, Connecticut and now resides in Warwick, Rhode Island. She is a former reporter for *The Waterbury Republican* and *The Waterburian*.

Nancy Collins Boardman is a middle school teacher with a degree in English. She was first published in the Northeast Journal in 1989 and most recently in *The Newport Review*. In 1998 she published *Let Me Introduce You to Helen Pierce*. She is the publisher and editor of a history publication in newspaper format ongoing since 1997, *The Swansea Record*.

Louis E. Bourgeois was born in New Orleans in 1970 and earned his B.A. at Louisiana State University and his MFA at The University of Mississippi. A three-time nominee for the Pushcart Prize, he has published hundreds of poems and stories worldwide. Currently, he is an instructor of literature and writing at Rust College in Holly Springs, Mississippi.

N.M. Brewka lives in Beverly, Massachusetts with her husband Tom Clark and has been published most recently by *The North American Review*, Small Fires Press, and Pudding House Press.

Helen Marie Casey is an award-winning writer whose work has appeared in numerous journals. Her first chapbook, a narrative series of poems about Joan of Arc, *Fragrance Upon His Lips*, was published by Finishing Line Press in 2005. Her work has appeared in, among others, the *Connecticut Review, Rosebud*, and *America*.

James Cihlar has worked in education and publishing for many years. His work has appeared in *Prairie Schooner, Bloom, The James White Review, Minnesota Monthly, Northeast,* and in the online journal *The Big Ugly Review.*

Michele F. Cooper is the first-place winner in the TallGrass Poetry Competition, second-place winner in the Galway Kinnell Poetry Competition, author of two books and numerous published poems, founding editor of the *Newport Review* and *Crone's Nest* literary magazines, and of a chapbook series, *Premier Poets.*

Chella Courington migrated west in 2002 with an economist and two cats and now teaches English at Santa Barbara City College. She returned to writing poetry in May 2003 after a lapse of twenty years.

Barbara Crooker has published in magazines such as *Yankee, The Christian Science Monitor,* and *The Denver Quarterly,* anthologies, including *Worlds in their Words: An Anthology of Contemporary American Women Writers,* and eleven chapbooks. Her first full-length book, *Radiance,* won the Word Press First Book award, and came out in 2005. She has absolutely no regrets about anything.

Jane D'Arista majored in English at Barnard College but has pursued a career as an economist for the U.S. House of Representatives and lecturer on international finance at Boston University and the New School University. She continues to write poetry in whatever time is available.

Jessica G. de Koninck's poems appear in a number of journals including *The Jewish Women's Literary Annual, Bridges* and *River King Poetry Supplement.* Her work has been nominated for a Pushcart Prize. A graduate of Brandeis University and an attorney by profession, she is Director for Legislative Services for the New Jersey Department of Education.

Julie R. Enszer is a writer and lesbian activist living in Maryland. She has previously been published in *Long Shot, Salt River Review, Room of One's Own, Technodyke.com, Push* (Seattle), *Suspect Thoughts* and *Iris: A Journal About Women.* Her work is forthcoming in *Poetry*

Fish and the *Harrington Lesbian Fiction Quarterly.*

Blanche Farley is a librarian at Middle Georgia College and lives in Dublin, Georgia. She is co-editor of *Like a Summer Peach: Sunbright Poems and Old Southern Recipes* (Papier-Mâché Press). Her work has been published in various journals, textbooks and anthologies including *Newsday Sunday Magazine, Kalliope, The Bedford Introduction to Literature* and *The Signet Book of American Humor.*

Jeremy William Farrington lives in Westchester, NY. He recently completed his MA in Creative Writing from Manhattanville College. In his spare time, he writes for www.sienafootball.org.

Audrey Friedman teaches 8th grade English in Rhode Island. She received an MFA in Poetry from Vermont College in 2005. Audrey's work appears in numerous literary journals including *The Comstock Review, California Quarterly, The Broad River Review,* and the *Newport Review.*

Alice Friman has new work in *Shenandoah, Gettysburg Review, Indiana Review, Prairie Schooner, Southern Review, Boulevard,* and others. Her book, *Zoo* (University of Arkansas Press, 1999), won the Ezra Pound Poetry Award from Truman State University and the Sheila Motton Prize from the England Poetry Club.

Lee Glantz of Barrington, Rhode Island is a batik artist and poet. Her writings have been published in *The Detroit Jewish News, West Crook Review, Muddy River Poetry Review, Crone's Nest,* the online magazine *RIRoads.com,* and in the book *Quarters of the Mind.*

Cecelia Hagen grew up Norfolk, Virginia and lives in Eugene, Oregon. Her poems have appeared in *Seattle Review, Prairie Schooner, Poet & Critic, Exquisite Corpse, Caffeine Destiny,* and elsewhere. Portland's 26 Books Press published her chapbook, *Fringe Living,* in 2000. She has received awards and fellowships from the AWP, Oregon Literary Arts, the MacDowell Colony, and Caldera Foundation.

Pat Hegnauer, Founding Director of 2nd Story Theatre, has been an acting teacher, producer, actress, director, and is now a playwright and poet. Her poems have been published in *Crone's Nest*, *Scrivener's Pen*, and *Wicked Alice*, among others. Her chapbook, *A Few Uncompromised Letters*, was published by the Premier Poets Chapbook series.

Cher Holt-Fortin grows tomatoes, makes quilts, considers herself a Southerner (partly), and has done aikido for 25 years.

Kake Huck is an Oregon poet who won the 2K3 poetry prize from The Peralta Press. She has published in *Ekphrasis, Harpur Palate,* and the anthology *Women's Encounters with the Mental Health Establishment.*

Roy Jacobstein's book of poetry, *Ripe*, was a finalist for the American Academy of Poets' Walt Whitman Award and won the University of Wisconsin's Felix Pollak Prize. His work has appeared in *The Gettysburg Review, The Threepenny Review, TriQuarterly* and other literary journals, and was nominated for the Pushcart Prize in 2002, 2003 and 2004. He is a public health physician working internationally on women's reproductive health.

Rhoda Janzen teaches creative writing at Hope College in Holland, Michigan. She has contributed poems to many literary journals, including *The Yale Review* and *The Gettysburg Review.* Her book *Babel's Stair* is forthcoming from Word Press.

Catherine McCrane Keating taught English and Drama in the Washington, DC public schools and at a woman's university in Tokyo, Japan. Her feature articles appeared in *The Washington Post* and *The Providence Journal,* among other newspapers. She won a National Endowment of the Arts Fellowship for Fiction in 2004 awarded through the Rhode Island State Council of the Arts.

Kathleen Kirk is an editor of *RHINO*, a literary annual. Her work has appeared in numerous journals and anthologies, including *After Hours, Alligator Juniper, Common Review, Folio, Spoon River Poetry, Inhabiting the Body* (Moon Journal Press, 2002), *E: The 2002 Emily Dickinson Awards Anthology* (Universities West Press, 2003), and *Her Mark.* She has work forthcoming in *Oklahoma Review, Poetry East, Seeding the Snow,* and *A Fine Frenzy,* an anthology of

Shakespeare poems from University of Iowa Press.

Teresa Joy Kramer's poetry has appeared in venues such as *Cicada,* *Open 24 Hours, Woman Made Gallery's Her Mark 2004* and the Gival Press anthology *Poetic Voices Without Borders.* Her book reviews have appeared in *Crab Orchard Review.* She directs the Writing Center at Central Washington University.

Judy Kronenfeld's work has appeared in many magazines and journals. She is the author of a book and chapbook of poetry, as well as a book on Shakespeare. Recent and forthcoming publications include a second chapbook, *Ghost Nurseries* (Finishing Line Press, 2005). She teaches in the Department of Creative Writing, UC Riverside, and is currently looking for a publisher for her second full-length collection of poems, *Small Truce with Oblivion.*

Kathryn Kulpa was born in Rhode Island. Her first book, *Pleasant Drugs* (Mid-List Press, 2005), was awarded the Mid-List Press First Series Award in Short Fiction. She has also been honored with the Florida Review Editor's Award in Fiction and a supplementary award in the Bridport Prize International Writing Competition. Three of her stories have been nominated for a Pushcart Prize.

Suzy Lamson's poems have appeared in a number of small press magazines throughout the United States. Her collection, *A Rose Between Her Teeth,* was published by Hanover Press in 1998.

Ruth Mark is a licensed psychologist, poet and editor. She is Irish but lives in the Netherlands where she teaches undergraduates about the workings of the brain. Her work has been published in diverse print and web venues including *Riviera Reporter, Dakota House Journal, Green Tricycle* and many more. More details can be found at: www.remark.be.

Lisa McMann lives and writes near Phoenix. She is the recipient of a 2004 Templeton Award for her short story, *The Day of the Shoes.* More of her published work can be found on her website, www.lisamcmann.com.

Judith H. Montgomery's poems appear in *The Southern Review, Gulf*

Coast, and *The Bellingham Review,* among other journals, as well as in several anthologies. Her work has received the National Writers Union and Americas Review poetry prizes; she has been awarded a Literary Arts Fellowship and a 2005 Oregon Arts Commission Individual Artist Fellowship. Her chapbook, *Passion,* received the 2000 Oregon Book Award. Her first full-length book, *Red Jess,* will appear in the February 2006. She holds a Ph.D. in American Literature from Syracuse University.

Kamilah Aisha Moon is a Cave Canem alumna, a Paumanok Award semi-finalist and an Emily Dickinson Award Honorable Mention. Her work has been featured in *Mosaic, Bittersweet, The Black Arts Quarterly, Open City, Phoenix, bum rush the page, Warpland, OBSIDIAN III* and *Toward the Livable City.* Moon is an MFA candidate at Sarah Lawrence College.

Deborah Narin-Wells has had poems published or forthcoming in *Poetry East, Poet Lore, Comstock Review, Southern Poetry Review* and many others. A chapbook, *Leaving Home,* is forthcoming from Traprock Books.

Lin Nulman's work has appeared in *The BlackWater Review,* in the online anthology *Tanka Splendor 2003* (AHA Poetry), and at swankwriting.com. She teaches at Bay State College in Boston and works in the theater whenever possible.

Susan Firghil Park is a former psychotherapist with degrees in psychology and counseling. Her poetry has appeared in *Spoon River Poetry Review, The Comstock Review, Branches Quarterly, West Wind Review* and *Tiger's Eye,* and recently won *The Alsop Review* poetry award. A chapbook manuscript, *La Muse Verte: Poems on the Life of Rimbaud* was a finalist in the 2004 Portlandia chapbook competition.

Meg Petersen teaches English at Plymouth State University and directs the Plymouth Writing Project. She is a founding editor of the Plymouth Writers Group Anthologies of Teachers' Writing, which is about to publish its tenth annual volume. She lives with her three sons in Plymouth, New Hampshire.

Helen Ruggieri lives in Olean, NY and teaches at the University of Pittsburgh, Bradford, PA. She has work in *Common Wealth*, an anthology of poems from Pennsylvania poets, and her book of short prose pieces, *The Character for Woman*, is available from foothillspublishing.com. Other work appears in *Cream City Review*, *Spoon River Poetry Review*, *Icon*, *Contemporary Haibun* and *World Haiku Review*.

Valerie M. Russo is a writer, poet and graduate student. She was born and raised in Spanish Harlem, NYC. She received her BA from Hunter College of the City University of New York. Once awarded the Langston Hughes Award for Writing, she currently works as a senior copy editor in the ever-unfaltering City of New York and is working on a novel.

Carly Sachs received her MFA from the New School University. She currently teaches creative writing at George Washington University. Her work has appeared in *Best American Poetry 2004*, *goodfoot*, *PMS*, *Another Chicago Magazine*, *No Tell Motel*, and on the buses of Cleveland, Ohio.

Joyce Sakala is an artist who lives and works in Newport, Rhode Island. She had been writing poetry for 5 years with the support and encouragement of the Newport Poets Society.

Shulla Sannella is a writer, poet and photographer living and working in northern Rhode Island. She has been published locally in *Crone's Nest*, *The Newport Review* and *4x4*. She is the author of two chapbooks, *Desire* and *Beach Poems*. "Writing is occupation, everything else I do is just preoccupation."

Laurence J. Sasso, Jr.'s poetry has appeared in more than 60 magazines and journals and has been recognized by a number of prizes and awards, including the Galway Kinnell Award and First Place in the Providence Journal Annual Poetry contest. Mr. Sasso is the author of *Harvesting the Inner Garden*, a chapbook. He served for seven years as poetry editor for The Providence Sunday Journal, and in the 1980s founded the journal *The Greyledge Review* with his late father. He was recently named Town Poet for Smithfield, Rhode Island.

Lawrence Schimel is an award-winning author and anthologist. His work has been translated into more than a dozen languages. He divides his time between New York and Spain, where he is the Regional Advisor for the Spain Chapter of the Society for Children's Book Writers and Illustrators.

Willa Schneberg received the 2002 Oregon Book Award in Poetry for her second collection *In the Margins of the World*. *American Poetry Review*, *Tikkun*, *Salmagundi*, and *Exquisite Corpse* are among the journals in which her poems have appeared. Her poem "Biscuits" was read by Garrison Keillor on the Nov. 20, 2002/2003 Writer's Almanac. Through Poetry-in-Motion, this spring, a snippet of her poem can be read on public transportation in the Portland, Oregon metro area. She worked for the U.N. in Cambodia from 1992-1993, during the U.N. sponsored election period.

Ada Jill Schneider is the author of two books of poetry: *Fine Lines and Other Wrinkles*, *The Museum of My Mother*, and the chapbook *Poems for Grandma and Me*.

Barbara Schweitzer's poetry has received numerous prizes including "Best Poem for 2002" by *Potpourri Magazine*, and a fellowship from RI State Council on the Arts. Her work is published in various literary and online journals and in the anthology *Sundays at Sarah's*. Her first collection of poetry 33 1/3, a semi-finalist for the Bakeless Prize, will be published in 2006 by Little Pear Press. She maintains a private psychotherapy practice in Providence, RI.

Elizabeth Scism's poetry has appeared in *ByLine*, *Chaffin Journal*, *Potomac Review*, *Lullwater Review*, and *Xavier Review*, among other journals. She teaches Creative Writing and American Literature in high school.

Suzanne Sigafoos, born and raised in the Midwest, studied acting and worked in the theater in her young artist days. After a thirty-year hiatus from creative pursuits, Suzanne was struck by the urge to write poems. She studies the craft of poetry and writes, grateful to be part of a vital community of poets and artists in Portland, Oregon, her home since 1999.

Angela D'Arista Solli, born in New York City and raised in the States, has been living in Europe for many years. Together with her writing career she has devoted her life to the study of the piano. She is married to an Italian engineer who has translated her poetry over the years.

Margo Solod has been an innkeeper, chef, lighting designer and factory worker to support her writing habit. After 20 years of traveling, 4 chapbooks, 90+ published poems in 70+ print and online magazines, 3 trucks and 9 sets of tires, she has settled in the middle of 72 acres in the Shenandoah Valley of VA. Her full length book of poems, *Graciously Allowed to Stay*, has just been released by may-apple press.

Elizabeth Stabler lives in Bristol, Rhode Island. Her poetry has appeared in *Crone's Nest*, *The Newport Review*, and *Shifts of Vision: An Anthology of Teachers' Writing* as well as in the chapbook *In this Moment...Another Glistens*.

Dianne Stepp lives in Portland, Oregon. She is a graduate of Warren Wilson College. Her chapbook, *Enchantment and Other Griefs* won the John and Miriam Morris Memorial award for 2005. Her poems have been published in numerous anthologies and journals including *Willow Springs*, *Calyx*, *The Sonora Review*, *Clackamas Literary Review*, *The Oregonian*, and ForPoetry.com.

Amanda Surkont's work has appeared in *Art Life*, *Concrete Wolf*, *The Nedge*, *Puckerbrush Review*, *The Newport Review*, *4 x 4*, *Pulse* and other journals. She is poetry editor at Rhode Island Roads Magazine. She lives in the Northeast Kingdom of Vermont.

Elizabeth Thomas is a published poet who designs and teaches writing programs throughout the U.S. An outstanding advocate of youth in the arts, she started UpWords Poetry, an organization dedicated to promoting programs for young writers. She is an organizer and coach of the Connecticut National Youth Poetry Slam team and hosts a website for young writers at www.upwordspoetry.com.

Shelley Ann Wake is a poet and short story writer from Australia. Her work has appeared in various Australian literary journals and several anthologies. While not writing, Shelley works as a business and marketing consultant and is currently completing a Masters in Advertising.

Davi Walder's poetry and prose have appeared in more than 150 publications including *The American Scholar, JAMA, Seneca Review, Lilith, Ms.,* and *Washington Woman.* Her latest collection of poetry, *Gifts,* was commissioned by the Milton Murray Foundation for Philanthropy. She received the 2002 Myrtle Wreath Award from the Hadassah of Greater Washington.

Chris Waters has been nominated for the Pushcart Prize in poetry and splits his time between Rhode Island and Cape Hatteras. His collection of poetry *Outer Banks Sonata* was published in 2004.

Gary J. Whitehead has authored one full-length collection of poems, *The Velocity of Dust* (Salmon Publishing), and two chapbooks, both winners of national competitions. He currently resides off the grid in the wilderness of Oregon as winner of PEN Northwest's Margery Davis Boyden Wilderness Writing Residency.

Elizabeth Whyman is 27 and lives in the North of England. She's had poems published in several U.K. magazines and works full-time for Mslexia, the bestselling U.K. magazine for women who write.

Christopher Woods is the author of a prose collection, *Under a Riverbed Sky,* from Panther Creek Press, and a collection of stage monologues for actors, *Heart Speak,* from Stone River Press. His play, *Moonbirds,* received its New York City premiere by Personal Space Theatrics. He lives in Houston.

Andrena Zawinski, a native of Pittsburgh, lives in Oakland, California where she teaches writing for Laney Community College and St. Mary's College. She is the award-winning author of a full-length collection of poetry, *Traveling in Reflected Light* (Pig Iron Press), a chapbook, *Andrena Zawinski's Greatest Hits 1991-2001,* and an online collection of Elegies at *The Pittsburgh Quarterly.* Her publications include *Gulf Coast* and *Quarterly West* among others.

About the Editor

Martha Manno is a fiction writer and editor. She founded Little Pear Press in 2003. She lives in southeastern Massachusetts.

Also available from Little Pear Press

Sundays at Sarah's:
An Anthology of Women's Writing
Go to www.littlepearpress.com.